GUARD YOUR MARRIAGE

Titilayo Akinniyi

Achievers Publishing Inc
Calgary, Canada

GUARD YOUR MARRIAGE
Copyright © 2014 By Titilayo Akinniyi

ISBN: 978-0-9918829-4-6

Published in Canada, by
Achievers Consult & Publishing Inc

Canadian Cataloguing in Publication (CIP)
A Record of this Publication is available from the Library and Archives Canada (LAC).

"The right of Titilayo Akinniyi to be identified as the author of this work has been asserted in accordance with the Copyright, Designs and Patents Act 1988 sections 77 and 78"

All rights reserved. Written permission must be secured from the publisher to use or reproduce any part of the book except for brief quotations in critical reviews, magazines or articles.

For further information or permission, address:
Achievers Consult & Publishing Inc
Calgary, Canada
E-mail: info@achieverspublishinghouse.com
www.achieverspublishinghouse.com

Printed in Canada for Achievers Consult & Publishing Inc

Dedication

"Guard Your Marriage" is a product of the Spirit of the Creator of heaven and earth. He is the giver of good and perfect gifts; my heavenly Father.

To Him alone I dedicate this book.

Acknowledgement

To my God and Redeemer, I say thank you.

To my husband, the crown of my head, I say thank you. You are indeed the God ordained helper of my destiny. You worked tirelessly through your words of encouragement to see this book written.

My wonderful gifts, the children that God blessed my marriage with, Oluwakemi, Olayinka and Oluwatobiloba Akinniyi, I say thank you. I thank God for making me the vessel through which you came to this world. It is a great honour. Thank you for your constant prayers and support.

I will forever be grateful to the Senior Pastors of Daystar Christian Center, Lagos Nigeria: Reverend Sam and Pastor Adenike Adeyemi for bringing out the golden treasures deposited by God in my life.

To my biological father, Mr Abass Olajire Lawal, whose marital challenge was my ready reference in this book, I am most grateful.

To my late mother, Mrs Samiat Lawal, who lived the life of an injured woman but still forgave, I offer my post-humus appreciation. Your last breath was in the same house where you were ill-treated. You were indeed a woman of great understanding.

My senior brother, I say thank you for your support with my education. God bless you.

It is my prayer that none of our children will experience the challenges that we went through while growing up in Jesus' mighty name.

Thank you all.

Table of Contents

Dedication	3
Acknowledgement	4
Table of Contents	6
Foreword	7
Chapter 1 - A Little Story	9
Chapter 2 - You Are the Caretaker of Your Home	12
Chapter 3 - Definitions of Marriage	17
Chapter 4 - Wrong Reasons for Getting Married	26
Chapter 5 - Right Reasons for Getting Married	38
Chapter 6 - Ingredients for a Successful Marriage	42
Chapter 7 - A man called Jairus	52
Chapter 8 - Appreciate Your Wife	59
Chapter 9 - Restoration for Your Marriage	63
Chapter 10 - Be a Home Builder	65
Chapter 11 - Add Value to Yourself	68
Confession for the Woman	76
Confession for the Man	77
Prayer of Salvation	78

Foreword

Writing the foreword for this book written by my sister, Mrs. Titilayo Akinniyi gives me such a pleasure and honour, and I will do it over and over again as the Lord gives her the privilege to write more books.

Within the few years that I have known this woman of God, I have noticed many things about her that serves as proofs of her qualification to undertake writing a book on Marriage and Home. She is a good example of someone who walks the talk. She is an iconic proverbs 31 woman.

Her husband is highly respected and her children are perfectly well behaved kids. I remember that at a youth camp organized by a church in 2013, her children were awarded the best behaved kids at the camp. That was not a co-incidence as she opens her mouth with wisdom, and always goes about doing God's work and serves as a role model for her children.

She is a dutiful wife and mother and loves God, her family and the family of God so much. I will highly recommend this book to every couple and would be couple. I could not afford to put the book down after I started reading it.

Note that, you are in for a life changing treat and encounter, reading this book. I am certain that your home and life will not remain the same after reading this book. God bless you richly as you embark on this insightful journey.

Mrs Adefolaju Adeniyi

Chapter 1

A Little Story

My parents both grew up in the sleepy town of Apomu in South-west Nigeria. They both came from low-income families.

Mother's junior brother, who was her companion in school, had died; so my grandparents stopped mother from finishing elementary school. For security reasons, my grandparents thought it was unwise to allow mother, being female, to continue to attend school all by herself after her brother's death. Since mother could not continue her education, she began trading. In those days, it was common for women who did not go to school to trade.

Father was more privileged because he had access to western education. His parents were Muslims but he had to teach in a Catholic School. At that time, you couldn't teach in a Catholic School unless you were a Catholic. So father became a Catholic. Teachers earned very little and since father's salary was not enough for him to "settle down", he decided to change job. He found a better paid job with the Nigerian Police Force.

Father met mother while he was still a teacher. They both fell in love but mother had to wait for father to finish his training at the Police College before they could be married. The waiting period paid off in the end. After the training, father and mother got married and less than a year later, they had a baby boy.

The first couple of years of marriage were very blissful for father and mother. The couple were so much in love that they both did their grocery shopping together at the end of every month. This was very unusual in those days. Society frowned at men helping out on what was considered "women's chores". But it was not long before the marriage which had started very well turned into what could be considered "hell on earth".

Mother was pregnant with her second baby (me) when tragic cracks started to develop in her relationship with father. Father had brought home a strange woman in a subtle way. He was the police officer assigned to handle a case involving this strange woman. Through a strange twist of events, it was not long before the woman became father's wife. Needless to say, a family feud started when the strange woman moved in as father's second wife. It was in the midst of the family feud that I was born on March 4, 1964.

Chapter 2

You Are the Caretaker of Your Home

I have a word of caution for men here - Make sure you put on your thinking and spiritual caps when dealing with strange women. The devil can creep in to your marriage at any point in time. God has positioned you as the caretaker of your marriage – make sure you manage it well.

It was through negligence that Adam lost his position as a caretaker. God made him the caretaker of the Garden of Eden and the beautiful woman that God gave him. But he got his head completely buried in the weed. He was so busy with the task of tending the garden and looking after the animals that he almost completely forgot Eve. Nature, we understand, abhors a vacuum. Satan quickly realized there was a gap between Adam and Eve. He saw the gaping opportunity in Adam's marriage and promptly crept in. A woman needs constant assurance that her husband is there for her. The moment there is reason for a woman to doubt her husband's support, the marriage is in danger. It will take God to put things right again. My father allowed a strange woman into his home and the course of his marital destiny changed. He still has not recovered from the consequences of that action up till now.

The Bible warns men never to deal unlawfully with the wife of their youth. Malachi 2:14. The reward of dealing unfaithfully with your wife is struggle and frustration. No man ever raises his hand to beat his wife and remains as successful as he should be. Success can be defined in many ways. It is not only in terms of money. How successful is a billionaire who does not have peace?

Men, be careful! The problems of the world are caused by men. If men will take responsibility for what God has committed into their hands as the heads of their homes, the world will be a better place to live.

The word of God tells us that the glory of children is their father.

Proverbs 17:6 says, *"Children's children are the crown of old men, and the glory of children is their father"*.

You will never realize the extent of the harm that is being done to your children when you leave the wife of your youth for a strange woman. You are helping to make the journey of their lives to be difficult and hard, which the Lord will ask you questions about. Remember Adam in the Garden of Eden. He was the first person that God contacted to find out what happened. God is watching. Proverbs 15*:3 says, "The eyes of the Lord are in every place, keeping watch on the evil and the good"*.

The beauty of a nation is preserved by the fathers. Men, do not allow your nation to be in ruins. Guard yourselves with God's wisdom; take us back to the beginning - the Garden of Eden. Glory has long disappeared from many homes because the fathers are not there. They left their God given assignments to follow strange women.

A man who sees himself as the saviour of the

world without first saving his family is a noise maker.

Any man who does not provide for his family is worse than an infidel (an unbeliever).

Provision is not only in monetary terms. It could be in the form of security - not giving your woman a home, but a house. There is great difference between a home and house.

The Bible says the sacrifice of the wicked is an abomination to the Lord.

Many prayers remain unanswered because of man's negligence of his duty at home.
Home is a place of safety, freedom and approval for the woman.
You do not have to live in a mansion before you have a home.
I remember when I wanted to get married to my husband. I asked him if he would give me a home as I never had one. When I was growing up, my parents provided me a house but not a home. I was deprived of a proper home.

As a man, be what God has designed you to be in your marriage.
You will be held responsible on judgement day.

Eve had no choice but to make friend outside her home in order to be happy. She chose the person who was available and caring.

If you care for your home, you will be available. We have many absentee fathers.

Chapter 3

Definitions of Marriage

Let us take a moment to understand what marriage is all about.

What is marriage?

1. Marriage is the union between a matured man and a matured woman. It takes a man and a woman who have the ability to respond to the environment in an appropriate manner according to dictionary definition of maturity, to have a successful home. Marriage has its own environment. Its environment is designed by God to be peaceful, loving, caring and conducive to the building of good character. All these were lost due to the fall of man.

   Thank God for a new beginning in Christ Jesus. He took it back for us on Calvary's tree. Some things, planned or unplanned, may influence or affect the marital environment; things like financial storm, health issues, fruit of the womb, friends and families.

   How these are handled depends on the

maturity level of the man or woman. How matured are you to enter into a marriage relationship. The wind of life will come. How prepared are you? Dealing with your spouse with maturity will help in recreating God's original plan for marriage in your home.

2. Marriage is a covenant union originated by God in the Garden of Eden. A covenant is a form of agreement between two people. It is a written promise between two individuals that frequently constitutes a pledge to do or refrain from doing something (the free dictionary.com).

Marriage is an agreement that both parties must be fully committed to for the full package of God's blessings to be released.
The Bible makes it clear that he that breaks a hedge, the serpent will bite. Ecclesiastes 10:8, says, *"He who digs a pit will fall into it, and whoever breaks through a wall will be bitten by a serpent"*.
When you enter into a marriage covenant, it is not only you and your spouse that are physically present at the ceremony. The God,

who instituted marriage, is right there with you and building a wall of protection round about you both. If you break the wall of protection through your disobedience, then you will be bitten by the serpent. This will not be your portion in Jesus' mighty name.

Not fulfilling your part of the covenant is an invitation to the serpent of troubles and chaos. This is what is happening now in our societies because of absentee fathers.

This covenant sometimes involves blood. When you have sexual relationship with your wife, you are cutting a blood covenant. 1 Corinthians 6:16 - 17 says, *"Or do you not know that he who is joined to a harlot is one body with her?*
For 'the two', He says, 'shall become one flesh'. But he who is joined to the Lord is one spirit with Him".

When you have sex with your spouse, you are saying whatever belongs to me belongs to you. When Jesus died on the cross, He shed his blood as a seal of our redemptive covenant, exchanging our sinful blood with His sinless blood and making us like Himself. That is why we can approach the throne of Grace with boldness. Remember, life is in the blood.

3. Marriage is an institution with God as the Teacher and the couple together with their children (if blessed with them) as the students. Every institution has a teacher or someone to put the students through their studies. It can either be virtual or physical.
Also in marriage, God is our teacher. We must have teachable spirit to be in this class of study. We must be prepared to learn all the way through in marriage.

We must be ready to do the assignments given by God to score a pass mark. We must be ready for group discussions with our spouse in the school of marriage.

4. Marriage is an institution with no graduation date. At all levels of secular education, there is a start date and an end date. In marriage, the program runs "till death do us part". When

you are married, you are married. In 1 Corinthians 7:10, Paul the Apostle says, *"Now to the married I command, yet not I but the Lord: A wife is not to depart from her husband"*. Verse 11 says, *"But even if she does depart, let her remain unmarried or be reconciled to her husband. And a husband is not to divorce his wife."*

Malachi 2: 16 *"For the Lord God of Israel says That He hates divorce,*
For it covers one's garment with violence,
Says the Lord of hosts.
Therefore take heed to your spirit,
That you do not deal treacherously."

5. Marriage is a place of continuous learning. You have to give yourself to continuous learning. No stopping. 1 Peter 3:7 counsels, *"Husbands, likewise dwell with them with understanding, giving honour to the wife, as to the weaker vessel, and as being heirs together of the grace of life, that your prayer may not be hindered"*.

It takes studying to have understanding. Get books on Godly marriage.

2 Timothy 2:15 says, *"Be diligent to present yourself approved to God, a worker who does not need to be ashamed, rightly dividing the word of truth."*

Read books that is about how to relate with the woman in your life. Remember, women are very different in many ways to men. Men are logical while women are intuitive. It takes time to fully understand who your wife is.

6. Marriage is an institution where you are allowed to enter through a door that has just one handle on the outside, there is no handle on the inside. In marriage, divorce in never in God's agenda for His children. Tell me how you will think of divorce when you are living with the best friend you could ever dream of having in life? Divorce is not on your mind when you sleep and wake up smiling every day. You do not think of divorce when your body is touching the best body you can think of on a daily basis. You certainly do not contemplate a divorce when you are sharing your most intimate moments with your own flesh and bone.

It will take someone out of his senses to think of divorce in the above circumstances. That is God's plan and purpose for every marriage. Malachi 2:16, *"For the Lord God of Israel says that He hates divorce, for it covers one's garment with violence, says the Lord of hosts".*

You see, there is just one handle to the marriage door. That is God's ultimate design.

7. Marriage is a place where all involved are subject to each other. Marriage involves more than one person, which makes it a team. So, teamwork as defined by Wikipedia.com is, "Work done by several associates with each doing a part but all subordinating personal prominence to the efficiency of the whole." Your wife's idea is as important as yours.

In Ephesians 5:22-25, wives are told to submit to their own husbands as to the Lord and husbands to love their wives as Christ loved the Church and gave Himself for her. I have heard someone say that you cannot say you respect or submit to your Pastor when you are not submissive to your own husband who is the prophet in your home. Also, if any man can give himself to his wife, he is in submission to his wife. That is what God wants. Successful marriage is a team effort.

8. Marriage is a life time journey; it is a life time commitment. As I said earlier, it has no exit door.

9. Marriage is a place of total commitment. According to Vocabulary.com, commitment means dedicating yourself to something or someone.

   Commitment in marriage is more serious than any other form of commitment that can easily be broken. If you take a job offer, it is your commitment that guarantees your pay.

   You need to think carefully before getting involved with a marital commitment. It will take a lot out of you. At the same time, maintaining your integrity in the affair brings its own eternal reward. Proverbs 22:23 says, *"Do you see a man who excels in his work? He will stand before kings; he will not stand before unknown men"*.

Commitment brings our marriage to the level of royalty.

In this age, many men want to be "Mr Somebody married to Mrs Somebody" just to show that they are responsible according to societal values. While many men live up to the standards of the society by getting married, they fail to live up to the tasks involved in a marriage.

Many ladies also are only interested in wearing the gold or diamond rings to show that they are very lucky to be called "Mrs X" or "Mrs Y".

Many get into marriage without the full knowledge of what the institution is all about. Knowledge is power. Be fully armed before signing the dotted lines of a marriage certificate. There is no point rushing into marriage and living through hell when you can take your time to enter it and live happily ever after.

Chapter 4

Wrong Reasons for Getting Married

There are many wrong reasons why some people enter into marriage covenant. A few of the common reasons are outlined below.

1. Way of escape from home. This is more for the woman. Many ladies think that the moment they get married, they are free to do what they want. This is a misconception because, as a married woman you are responsible for home building. In fact the test of your character will come up. Remember, you are not just getting married to a man who dropped from heaven without a family. Relationship with some in-laws could be so frustrating. Women will easily understand what I mean. Some in-laws are just not easy to please.

No matter what you do, some in-laws don't see you as part of the family. They see you as a stranger from nowhere who has come to snatch what belongs to them. Think twice before you say "I do".

Are you ready emotionally and spiritually? Your answer will determine if you are in that relationship for the wrong or right reason.

2. Empathy. This is when you get married to someone because of pregnancy or because you feel so sorry for him or her due to past failed relationship.

Marriage is an eye opener. During courtship, you may be blinded, but immediately you exchange the marriage vows, your eyes will be opened if you did not open your heart to God for directions in the first place.
Marriage is to be enjoyed and not to be endured.
God's kind of marriage is entered into with both eyes open.

I got married as an unbeliever but I was very sure that there was a God in heaven who granted the desires of His children. I remember how I almost walked into a marriage with a married man several years ago. This man carefully concealed from me, the fact that he was married. But I was so trusting and unsuspecting. I never knew this man had three children and was still married.

Women, be careful in your relationship! This man would come to my school at least once a week to check on me. I took that as a demonstration of his love and care for me. All his brothers were so close to me and there was no way I could have suspected that he was married.

I was at his parents' home one weekend and saw a photo album. The first page I opened had the traditional wedding photo of a couple. I looked very closely at the photograph and noticed the striking resemblance between my fiancé and the groom. When I pointed this out, my fiancé quickly told me that the groom in the photograph was his uncle. I was so stupid to believe that. But this was because members of the family looked very much alike. I was fooled.

This relationship went on until God used my

fiancé's junior brother (he is now a pastor serving God) to reveal the truth to me. I remember this God-sent saviour came to my school while I was preparing for my semester exam. He said 'Mama T', (that was the name my fiancé's family fondly called me), "can you get me some beer to drink?" My prompt answer was "No". He then said, "A normal person can only behave like a mad man when he is intoxicated". Just as I was wondering why he made the statement, he quickly added that I should ask his senior brother about his marital life when next he came to see me. I said, "did you mean how your brother and I are going to plan our lives together?" He said no. That was when it dawned on me that I was on the wrong track.

One thing I will continue to be grateful to God for is the open heart He gave me even as an unbeliever. I see everyone I come across as a friend to care for. This was my saving grace. My fiancé's junior brother made a statement that I will never forget. He said "You have been so good to every one of us and it will be so unfair for me to keep this secret from you".

It was a big blow to me but my Heavenly Father turned it around to be a way to a very bright and great destiny for me. To Him alone be all the glory.

When God has a purpose for you, there is nothing He cannot do to establish that purpose.
God preserved me from the trap of the deceiver and gave me the best gift any woman could think of in the person of my husband Olusegun Oluwasogo Akinniyi.
God is a faithful God. Deuteronomy 7:9 says, *"Therefore know that the Lord your God is God. A faithful God..."*

I tell young ladies when counselling that if I, Titilayo, can marry a good man like my husband, as an unbeliever, then they should expect greater and better husbands. *"The latter shall be better than the former",* says Haggai 2:9.

Put your hope in God alone. I always tell my children never to put their priority in money or material things. Money has wings. If you marry a man because of his social status, one day this may not be there anymore. Every man has a seed planted by God in them to be successful.

God placed the seed of creativity in Adam. Adam named all the animals in the Garden of Eden because of the spirit of creativity deposited in him by God.

I got married to my husband when he was a lecturer at the University of Jos, though we had met when he was lecturing at the Civil Engineering department of the Federal Polytechnic Ilaro, Ogun State Nigeria where I was a student.

I tell you, I was not looking for anything but a home. Note that I said a "home" and not a "house".

To the glory of God we are where we are today by His grace. To Him alone be all the glory. From the obscurity of the little town of Apomu in Oshun State Nigeria, God lifted me up and took me to higher grounds in foreign nations. It can only be God.

Above all, God gave me the best that any living creature could desire - the gift of new birth. I got to know God because of my marriage.

I became relevant to my generation because of my God-ordained husband.

While I was yet a sinner, Christ died for me. What a privilege and honour.

What is it that God cannot do?

In God there is no useless situation.

Ladies, materials will go, it is your character that will remain.

3. Rebound. This is when you get married because of a failed relationship.

You want to prove to people or the other party involved that you are still marketable. Be careful! Notwithstanding the terrible experience I had with my fiancé in the failed relationship, I still had to do due diligence before saying "Yes" to my husband when he proposed to me. In fact, marriage was almost a thing that I never wanted to be involved in after the failed relationship.

I remember telling my father that I was no longer interested in getting married if a married man with children could be in a relationship with another woman for two years and not minding what this woman (his wife) went through in the labour room three times putting her life on the line to have his children. That is wickedness.

The wife does not have to curse him, that type of man is cursed already. The Bible warns man not to deal treacherously with the wife of his youth. Malachi 2:13-15.

When my husband proposed to me, I requested some of my male classmates, who knew about my failed relationship, to help me investigate his past relationships before I gave him a "Yes" answer.

"Once bitten, twice shy", goes the common saying. You do not have to be bitten by the wickedness of this world if you are conscious of your help in God.

I was an unbeliever then and lacked parental guidance.

But with God all things are possible. Ladies put on your "Caution Gear". Not every man you see is "husband material" and every woman you meet on the road cannot not be "wife material". Perhaps I should say, "not every man or woman that looks like it, is it". Seek God's face for His perfect choice for you.

4. Pressures from parents and friends. Never give in to pressures from anyone. Remember none of them will help in feeling the pain of a wrong choice when troubles start.

   Let God be your Lead. It does not matter if all your friends are getting married and you are still single. There is an appointed time for everyone. Your time is coming too.

   There is the ripe time for every fruit. A fruit plucked unripe does not taste sweet. The real sweetness of a fruit comes out when it is fully ripe and willing at God's ordained time to fall off the branch of the tree where it has been hanging for maturity.

If you allow people's opinion to drive you into a premature relationship, the same people will help you hire a U Haul Truck to pack up your marriage. That will not be your portion in Jesus' mighty name.

The Bible advises us never to make a vow in a hurry. Take time and think deep on what you are about to do.

Parents, do not be an instrument for the brokenness of lives. Some parents want to show their friends that they are good parents by making their children get married. Our children's marriages should not be turned to a status symbol for Christ's sake!

Do not get me wrong, it is every parent's prayer for their children to get married. It is more pleasant and loving when we allow God to direct these children on this matter. I think the best any parent can do is to take up the job of intercession on the behalf of their children.

We are most of the time afraid or impatient when our children, especially the females, go past what society considers to be marriageable age.

God said in His word that *"none of them will lack her mate",* Isaiah 34:16. When God says a thing, He has said it. God does not say one thing and then "un-say it" or deny it at the same time.

The Bible says in Genesis 1:27, *"So God created man in His own image; in the image of God He created him; male and female He created them".* The Bible says, *"male and female".* That is, for every man, there is a woman for him. We only need to open our eyes to see.

"He who finds a wife...", says the Bible in Proverbs 18:22. There is the finding that must be done.

Isaiah 50:8-11 tells us that God's ways and thoughts are totally different from ours. *"Commit your works to the Lord, and your thoughts will be established."* Proverbs 16:3.

Which is better? To mislead them and have sleepless nights looking for solution to their marital problems or to pray ahead and allow them to follow God's directions for them and sit down with our legs crossed as we see them blossom in their marriage.

I will definitely go for the latter. I want to see my children and their spouses sitting on thrones in my life time with my husband by my side. Life is so sweet.

Which woman would not want to be like President Obama's mother-in-law?

Good job mama. You deserve it. Enjoy the White house. God bless you Ma!

Chapter 5

Right Reasons for Getting Married

Just as there are wrong reasons for getting married so there are right reasons.

God instituted marriage for the following reasons.

1. **Companionship**. Genesis 2:18 says, *"And the Lord God said, 'It is not good that man should be alone; I will make him a helper comparable to him' "*. Adam was surrounded by the animals that God created but he was still lonely. He felt incomplete until Eve was brought to him and he was filled with so much excitement that he exclaimed, "...the bone of my bone and the flesh of my flesh". Marriage destroys the yoke of loneliness in our lives if we let God choose for us. It gives us our own friend.

   A friend that is closer than a brother. It creates avenue for team work and greater achievements in life. Quality decisions are made in marriage. Ecclesiastes 4:9-12 says, *"Two are better than one because they have a good reward for their labour..."*

2. **Procreation**. After creating man, God said, "be fruitful and multiply..." The seed of multiplication in Adam was reserved for Eve to bear Godly children. Until the arrival of Eve, Adam was going about with the seed in his body without any fruitful result. Getting married is an avenue for your God-given fruit producing seed to manifest its potential.

3. **For Godly seed.** The Bible says, *"God seeks Godly seed".* Malachi 2:15. He is looking for seeds that will be taught the way of God and will subsequently extend it to many generations. God's design for our children is to know Him, and introduce Him to others. This is His multiplication agenda.

4. **For Worship**. To worship is to show a lot of love and adoration for something or someone. Worship is an extreme form of love; it is a type of unquestioning devotion. If you worship

God, then you love God so much that you don't question him at all. Going to church is a form of worship, so is prayer (Vocabulary.com)

The reason for the creation of man is to worship God.

God was enjoying the worship of Adam alone in the cool of the day in the Garden of Eden and more from the two after Eve was created.

The reason for the deliverance of the children of Israel from the bondage of Pharaoh was for them to worship Him. Exodus 9:1.

"Then the Lord said to Moses, Go in to Pharaoh and tell him, 'thus says the Lord God of the Hebrews, Let My people go, that they may serve Me' ".

Service is a form of worship.

He wants husband and wife to worship Him and have Him as the pinnacle of their lives and marriage.

Our relationship with God in marriage can be illustrated by a triangle sitting on its base. The husband and wife are at the base looking up unto God who sits at the apex of the triangle as the only source of everything in their lives. This is also an act of submission to

God. The Bible says, *"If your eyes be single, the whole body will be full of light"*, Matthew 6:22.

Having our gaze on Him gives light to every situation in our marriage.

Never look unto your parents or friends. Most times, human beings are limited in their abilities to counsel. God is the only one who has the answers to all our marital questions.

"They looked unto Him and their faces were radiant and they were not put to shame", Psalms 34:5. There is no shame in Christ Jesus.

He is the only God who beautifies.

Chapter 6

Ingredients for a Successful Marriage

The success of a marriage depends on a number of factors.

1. **The headship of the marriage.**
   God is the supreme head of all. He created all things, marriage inclusive. When God is the number one in your marriage, nothing can derail your home.

   God is the pinnacle of the marriage triangle. Having the man and the woman at the base represents their submission to the leadership of God. As you draw closer to God your maker, the distance at the base of the triangle closes up and you both become one or a single line, still with God at the tip. Now your lives, goals, purpose, and affection are intertwined.

   Vision becomes "our vision" instead of "my vision".

Proverbs 12:7 says, *"The wicked are overthrown and no more, but the house of the righteous will stand"*.

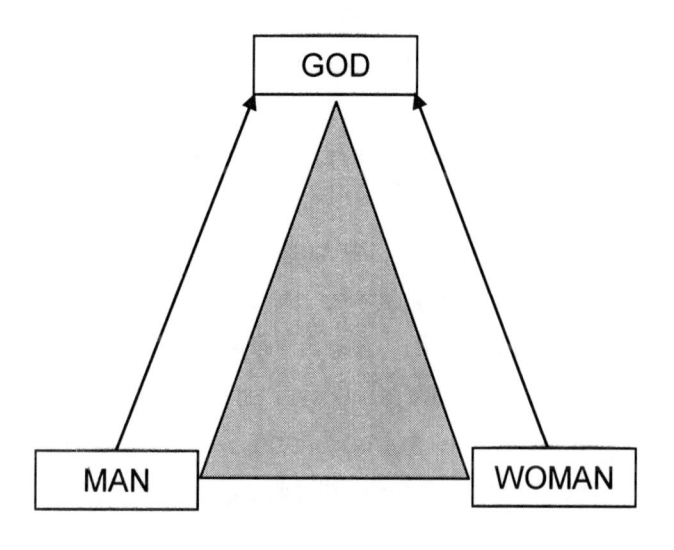

Figure 1: The Marriage Triangle

2. **Commitment**. Commitment in marriage is all about being sold out for the success of the union. It is not conditional; come rain or shine, you are completely in it.

   The sun of life will come in different ways. It could be for joy or the opposite. How committed you are to your marriage will determine how stable it will be.

When the rain of life comes, the foundation of your commitment will determine how well your marriage will stand.

Love may fade but commitment will not. The butterfly feelings in you during courtship will cool off, but commitment will ignite it again.

3. **A servant's heart**. Marriage is a call to servant hood. *"Let him who wants to be the leader be the servant of all..."*, Mark 9:35 Render services to each other. Make life comfortable for one another. A servant sees to the comfort of his or her master. When you serve your spouse and he/she serves in return, your home will be full of comfort.

If you see yourself as a servant to your spouse, there will be less strife in the home. If you realise that each one of you is to help one another to achieve your God-given assignments, there will be no need for competition between husband and wife. We are not rubbing shoulders but walking side by side to greatness together. Nothing can be achieved except it has been given from above.

Remember we are to complement each other. We are to walk side by side holding each other's hand to success.

4. **Forgiveness**. Forgiveness is a vital ingredient of a successful marriage. No one is perfect, we are only walking towards perfection.

We are all work in progress. To see ourselves as faultless is wrong. When your spouse upsets you, be ready to forgive. Forgiveness does not translate to keeping quiet without telling your spouse what makes you feel bad.

When a problem is bottled up for too long in the bid for peace, there will come a time when the bottle will lift up its lid and spill out the dirty contents which may be too late or difficult to clean up.

Forgiveness opens up our heavenly blessings for our marriage.

5. **Openness**. Be open to each other. Be free to say it as it is. Nothing is hidden.

What you think is hidden will be made known one day in the open. Shame and disgrace may be the reward.

Adam and Eve were both naked and were not ashamed. It does not mean nakedness as in having sex. It means in the things affecting each person.

What ordinarily cannot be said outside the home is made known between the two.

Transparency is the key. There should be nothing in the dark.

6. **Communication**. This is to marriage as blood is to life. A home with little or no communication is heading for the ditch. A "communication-less" home is a lifeless home. If you were travelling by train and all of a sudden the train stopped and nothing was communicated to the passengers by the driver everybody would be confused. Lack of communication brings confusion in marriage. It must be clear and precise. It is through communication that knowledge is transferred and issues are dealt with in love. You are able to express your feelings toward each other through communication. Making love is a form of communication.

Communication is two-way and an art. You need to learn how to communicate effectively. Lack of effective communication between Adam and Eve was what led to the fall of man. The Last Adam, our Lord Jesus Christ, knew who He was in God the Father when the tempter, the devil, came in Matthew 4:6. The Bible says in verse 6, *"and said to Him, if you are the Son of God, throw Yourself down. For it is written: 'He shall give His angels charge over you...' "*

Jesus answered back with the right answer according to what God said. He heard God clearly about who He, Jesus, was in God. No ambiguity of information.

Many men have forgotten what God told them about the woman in their lives and took what people said.

They dwell in what their feelings say or what their parents say. Nothing is written on the tablets of their hearts concerning the plans of God for their marriage. Proverbs 1:5-6 says, *"A wise man will hear and increase learning and a man of understanding will attain wise counsel".*

What are you learning? Whose counsel are you taking? How wise are you in your communication pattern with your spouse? Learn to listen to what she has to say. Do not shut her down before you hear what she is trying to tell you. Many times women do not need your solution, all a woman wants is your support. Knowing that you are there to listen to her.

Be a man of understanding and attain wise counsel.

Women love to be talked to in special ways, and same goes for men.

Take time to understand how your wife wants to be communicated to. Learn her love language. It could be by touching, by words of affirmation, by buying her gifts or just hugging. Women are moved by actions, it is not enough for you to assume "she should know I love her".

Rev. Sam Adeyemi said he would buy something for his wife everyday on his way home from work. Things as little as one cent sweets. I tell people to buy for their spouses whatever they can afford, no matter how little, as long as it is tagged with their spouse's name. Your spouse knows that it is a matter of time; that little thing will become bigger. What you are doing is communicating your love to her.

7. **Sex**. This is a powerful tool for a successful marriage.

   Strife, quarrels or disagreements are often ended through sex. Sex is designed to create bond between husband and wife. This is where the two spirits are knitted together. Learn the art of sex. Invent new styles. Do not always go, "as it was in the beginning, so shall it be" style. You do not always have to switch off the lights or have sex in bed or in a particular position. Be creative, ladies!

   Be your husband's wife and mistress. Have you ever wondered why married men go to harlots or have girl friends outside their marriage? Read what the crafty harlot said in Proverbs 7:16-17. How well made is your matrimonial bed? What smell is coming out of your room and body? Is it the type that kills the sexual appetite of your husband?

The crafty harlot really invested in some things to deceive the foolish man. If an unbeliever would go the extra mile to take away men from believers, I think it is time for us to do away with mediocrity in our sex life.

A man who is sexually satisfied by his wife will not look for alternatives outside.

Men love sex. That is their second food. Give it to him and see if the next cheque will not be an open one.

You will hear him singing and running home all the time.

Your body is no longer yours the moment you say "I do" in marriage.

Never use sex as punishment for your spouse. It is ungodly.

If you do not enjoy having sex, pray and ask the Holy Spirit to help you love and enjoy it with your husband. God watches when you are having sex. He created it in the first place.

So, sex is holy in the context of marriage. Some women are the authors of their divorce papers. They neglect the men by not looking good or cooking food that will make their man run home.

Put on sexy night wear. Keep fit and smell sweet.

8. **Love**. This is the feeling of belonging to one another. This may grow thin or fluctuate as the marriage advances, but the love of God will stand and stay strong all through.

Marriage is the bedrock of nations. A strong nation, is a nation with solid family life.

A nation with troubled family will inevitably have no peace and will experience an unstable economy.

The future of a nation depends greatly on the stability of the family.

Seeds (children) from an unstable marriage are often the initiators of the destruction of a nations resources.

Chapter 7

A man called Jairus

Let us look at the life of the man called Jairus. Luke 8:40-42; 49-56

Verse 40: *"So it was, when Jesus returned, that the multitude welcomed Him, for they were all waiting for Him".*

Verse 41: *"And behold, there came a man named Jairus, and he was a ruler of the synagogue. And he fell down at Jesus' feet and begged Him to come to his house, for he had an only daughter about twelve years of age, and she was dying".*

The name Jairus means, "Dispersal of light", which in my own opinion means, that this man was a man that was full of knowledge and understanding.

He was a ruler. Someone in a position of authority. A fool cannot be a ruler in Israel. A man who is void of knowledge and good understanding of how to rule his house cannot be in a high position in Israel, I believe. This man was in constant touch with his family despite his position in the country. A lot of leaders in our society have long forgotten what family life is all about. Their main concern is their political career, forgetting the family.

Jairus was so much in tune with his family that he knew when things went wrong with his only daughter.
Some men are so ungrateful to God that they even despise their female children.
A lot of men in Jairus' position would leave the care of the home and children to the women. It should have been the woman running here and there to see that the girl received medical care. The Bible says, *"And behold, there came a man named Jairus..."*

Jairus came to Jesus to seek solution to a problem in his home. In so many churches, the population of women is more than the population of men.
Many men do not have time for God. Most of the time, you will only see women in prayer gatherings.
This man was an exception. He showed that he was truly a ruler of his home.
He came to Jesus and fell down at Jesus' feet and begged.

He did not see himself as too high up in government to fall down and worship Jesus.

"Before honour is humility" - Proverbs 15:33b
Jairus humbled himself so that his daughter could be raised up by Jesus.

Many men need to bend down at the feet of Jesus for good to come their way. Many Christians are too conscious of their titles, even in the church, and cannot bend down or kneel at His feet to beg on behalf of their loved ones.

This man was not ashamed of the multitudes watching. He was not conscious of his attire. He fell down and begged.

As he was begging, there was an interruption by someone who touched Jesus and Jesus' attention was focused on something else.
Jairus did not give up. Even, one of his servants told him not to bother Jesus for the daughter had died. He was not moved.
Challenges will come in marriage. Distractions will come. People will try to intrude into our marriages. It is the determination of the

individuals involved that will make all these to be of no effect in their marriage, especially the man.

If the man of the house is filled with the knowledge of God and the plan and purpose of God for their marriage, challenges will become the platform for their lifting in their marriage. Jairus knew where to go for solution when challenges came in the form of ill health for his only daughter. He did not seek the counsel of others but of God.

The man is the prophet of his home. It is what you see and say as the prophet of your home that come to be.

Invite Him the institutor of marriage to your home at all times. And enjoy the healing that follows. Jairus' daughter was brought back to life because he invited Jesus to his house. What was dead came back to life!

Every dead relationship will come back to life in Jesus' mighty name.

Where are the Jairuses of today?

Most of them have gone after strange women. Jairus was available for his marriage to be successful. He went to seek solution for his child's sickness when other fathers were running after destruction in the form of strange women. My father, with the backing of his mother and sisters took in a strange woman and that brought his marital bliss to an end. There was no single day without chaos in the house.

The once peaceful home turned to an object of mockery in the neighbourhood. People would gather to watch two wives abusing each other and engaging in physical fight. It was a show of shame. Who was the culprit of all these? - The man.

The Bible says in Proverbs 4:23, *"Guard your hearts with all diligence for out of it are the issues of life"*.

Broken marriages lead to broken destinies. From broken homes come broken children with broken future and broken societies. It can only take God to mend their lives as He did mine. My life is a testimony of whom God has predestined before the foundation of the earth. Romans 8:28-30.

All I can say is "God I Thank You".

I think men who handled their marriages carelessly should be severely punished because they are the cause of the pains the society is going through.

The Bible says, *"God seeks Godly children"*, Malachi 2:15. What some men are giving God now is far from Godly children.

Malachi 2:10-11 says, *"Have we not all one father? Has not one God created us? Why do we deal treacherously with one another by profaning the covenant of the fathers?"* Verse 11 says, *"Judah has dealt treacherously, and an abomination has been committed in Israel and in Jerusalem, for Judah has profaned the Lord's holy institution which He loves, he has married the daughter of a foreign god"*.

A strange woman is a daughter of a foreign god. God was talking to men. He was not talking to women. Marriage is the heartbeat of God. Please, men, consider the way you handle your marriages.

Do not allow God to cut you off from His glorious promises.

Be satisfied with your wife. Have her to the fullest, especially when it comes to sex.

A satisfied soul loathes the honeycomb. But to a hungry soul every bitter thing is sweet. Proverbs

27:7.

Be filled with affection for your wife and you will loathe every form of strange woman.

Do not be a man who cannot control his sexual instinct and to whom everything in skirt is good enough. Be careful!

Chapter 8

Appreciate Your Wife

Eve was appreciated by the devil.
Appreciate your wife anytime she does something for you, the children or even for herself. That gives her more energy to move forward. Do not trash her opinion. Never make her feel irrelevant. She is not irrelevant in God's hand.

Eve was assured of her beauty by a stranger. How often do you notice your wife's change of hairdo or lipstick colour or outfit? The devil was so clever to touch all these areas in Eve's life. She trusted him completely. No wonder when the devil told her to eat the fruit, there was not much argument. She was even convinced to give it to her husband.

She went through training with the devil. She was engaged in communication with the devil, which she lacked in her own home. Be mindful of what is going on in your wife's life. Listen to what she says. It may not make sense to you at that particular time, take time to think about it. No woman is senseless. It will take a senseless man to marry a senseless woman.

The Bible says we should never say *"Raca"* to anyone, Matt 5:22. No woman is foolish. Eve was able to laugh and express herself anytime she was with the strange man (the devil). What are you doing with your wife? How much of your time do you spend with her? How many times do you assure her that she is the most precious gift given to you by God? How often do you bring out the little girl in her? Women are moved by words of appreciation and are security conscious.

You need to assure her that she is secure. I was looking for what was lacking in my life. I never had a home. I did not even have a house. Many people were bold to say my house but I did not have any.

Do you call a place where chaos is the order of the day a home?
Or a place where you do not have a room to put your things or a bed to sleep on at age 25? Men, give your children hope in life.

It is a different thing if due to lack of money, you could not do so much. When it is because of your stupidity and selfishness then, you will have yourself to blame in the future.

These children are aware of what is going on, do not be deceived. When the time comes, they will take proper care of their mother and you will be left alone.

My father can testify to this. He lives with the consequences of his costly mistakes till now.

Watch it and tread carefully.

Handle with care the precious gift God has given you.

"He who finds a wife, finds a good thing and obtains favour from the Lord". Proverbs 18:22.

Your favour from God is tied to your wife. Your greatness in life is tied to your wife. A married man is a blessed man.

Treat your wife with dignity and your destiny will be dignified.

Be faithful to your wife no matter what the pressure may be from family or friends. A husband who delights in maltreating his wife will also delight in shame and disgrace in the end.

The Bible says, *"One will chase a thousand and*

two will put ten thousand to flight", Deuteronomy 32:30. That is the mystery of the synergy between husband and wife. It is not possible to put ten thousand to flight when your wife is hurting.

My prayer is that God will raise many Jairuses in our generation in Jesus' name.

Chapter 9

Restoration for Your Marriage

A clarion call to all men - God is calling you to give you a new beginning.

It is never too late.

It is God's plan for humanity that every home or family should enjoy His marvellous light.

God gave every man a measure of light. John 1:4 *"In Him was life, and the life was the light of men."*

Jairus dispersed His God-given light to his family.

He was there to share the grief of his family and went all out to seek solution in the right place.

Many men are seeking solution to their marital problems in the wrong places with wrong associations. No one else can love your marriage more than you do.

You are the prophet in your home. Fathers, return to your family. Imagine if all men were Jairuses!

Every marriage in the world would be full of God's lights and nations would dwell in love with each other.

You can be the Jairus in your family by first reconnecting with the One who instituted marriage in the first place. Invite Him to your home.
Tell Him that the "wine" in your home is finished and watch how He is going to give you "new wine" in your marriage.

I pray for that woman whose husband has abandoned because of a strange woman - the hand of the Almighty will touch and heal you in Jesus' mighty name. There is a balm in Gilead - the balm of healing. Forgive and let God. That is the beginning of healing.

Un-forgiveness closes the heaven over us. Woman, remember you are wonderfully and fearfully made by your father in heaven. You are blessed and highly favoured in Jesus' mighty name.

Chapter 10

Be a Home Builder

I would like to say a word or two to the woman in this man's life.

Proverbs 14:1 says, *"The wise woman builds her house, but the foolish pulls it down with her hands".*

How wise are you in your marriage? Remember one of the definitions of marriage - a covenant relationship between a matured man and matured woman.

A lot of women are not matured in wisdom enough for marriage. If you lack wisdom in marriage, there is tendency for you to not build your marital home properly. In fact you may be the person that is pulling it down with your own hands.

The Bible says, *"submit to your own husband",* Ephesians 5:22. Many women submit to their friend's advice or to the man outside.

Many people submit to their career and business. Many women are too busy to care for their husband, the head of the home after God.

When he says one thing, you say twenty things. When it is time for sex, you always have issues to bring up. That is when you remember what he did wrong many months ago and now is the time to punish him by denying him sex.

A man who is not properly fed in the house will fall into the hands of a strange woman.

A man who is not respected at home by his wife will find solace outside. Every man craves for respect. Even a man without a penny or a cent to his name still wants to be respected by his wife.

Be his number one cheer leader. You are the number one subject in his kingdom. Do not talk to your husband anyhow. Learn to know what to say, how to say it and when to say it. Proverbs 25: 11, says, *"A word fitly spoken is like apples of gold in settings of silver".*

Study your husband's reactions when you are talking outside among friends and families. Be his queen at all times. Minister to him. I know a woman who said anytime she went to a party with her husband, she made it her duty to see that her husband was served the best food available. She would go to the food serving point and get her husband's food first. That is a queen indeed taking care of her king.

I heard Pastor Funke Felix-Adejumo saying that she normally reserves the best portion of meat in the soup pot for her husband and every morning, she kneels down to greet her husband after greeting God.

Tell me why the man will not love his wife. Which husband will be enjoying all these and go to a strange woman?

Women. Let us be the builders of our own homes and not the foolish ones that pull down marital homes with their hands.

Chapter 11

Add Value to Yourself

Many women need to add value to themselves in many areas.

1. **Outlook**. Some women think the moment they are married to a man, that is it. No need to look smart and beautiful any more especially after having one or two children. They think the man is tied to them. I have news for you.

   It is better to reinvest in your outlook. The way you dress is the way you will be addressed. If you dress shabbily, your husband will treat you shabbily by going out to look for a smart woman.

   Stop tying a wrapper around your chest at home looking like his grandma.

   Put on something smart always. Look good and smart. Do not forget that this man works outside the home and he sees so many beautiful women out there including smart secretaries.

Let your husband's eyes be full of good things before he leaves for work.

2. **Good body smell**. Women secrete some kind of smell due to many things going on in their bodies - the arm pit and private part especially during the monthly period. You need to be conscious of these and get the appropriate perfume.

A woman said, "If you do not like me, you will like my perfume".

I love good smell. I love when someone passes by me and the smell of her perfume lingers for a while.

I remember one day I was returning home from work in London, United Kingdom. At the train station, a lady passed by me and the perfume she was wearing was so good. I went to meet her and politely asked for the name of the perfume she used.

Since that day, I too started using that perfume as one of my favourite perfumes.
I like men who smell good and I make sure my husband gets the best I like.

Find out the perfume that your husband likes on a woman. Study his reaction to smell. Both good and bad. Make changes if needed. Do not take your husband for granted in this matter.

3. **Good food**. A woman who knows how to cook good food will always have the man's attention. The way to a man's heart is through his stomach.

In the book of Genesis 18:6-9, God asked for Sarah and promised her a child after Abraham had fed the three men who visited him.

It was the venison prepared for Isaac by Jacob that earned him the blessing which was not intended for him.

If you give your husband good food to eat, he will surely stay at home. Some men are so used to their wife's good food that they find it so difficult to eat outside the home. I salute such good women who keep their husband with good food.

If you do not know how to cook delicious meal

or variety of foods, go online and learn. There are so many recipes online or better still go to catering school and add value to your cooking skill.

There are different ways or form of how to eat rice, eggs and even potatoes.

You too can invent menus. The great cooks that we have today started somewhere. Try out some things and you will discover it is easy to become a celebrity chef in your home.

4. **Clean environment**. There is this saying that, "Cleanliness is next to Godliness". In the book of Exodus 19:10-11, God instructed the children of Israel to wash themselves for three days because He wanted to visit them. See, God does not like untidiness or unclean environment.

If your house is clean, it will be easy for fresh air to circulate and you will enjoy good health. Every man is proud to bring in friends and colleagues to their home when they are sure the house is clean and tidy.

Why do we have to start cleaning or tidying up every time a visitor is coming to our home.

We want to present ourselves as decent people.

It is better to live a tidy life rather than taking an emergency approach each time a visitor is coming to our home.

A tidy home is a man's delight. A wise woman will see to it that the home is well organised and welcoming.

One of my daughters made a remark one day when we had the opportunity to visit a family friend's home. She said "mum, I now know why this man (a pastor) normally rushes home after church service". I asked her why? She said, "did you not see how well decorated his house is?" She said she too would run home if our house was in such condition. I said that was very true. I agreed with her totally. That home was very tidy; everything was well placed with the colour combination skills of an expert interior designer.

Some homes are neglected by women but the men are looking for a neat environment.

Every home may not be as well organised as the one my daughter loved but the little we can do goes a long way.

Clean bedroom, kitchen and washroom is highly important.

You should be able to eat in your washroom. Some wealthy people have a sofa in their washroom.

There are so many types of air fresheners in stores that are not expensive. There are perfumed candles that you can use after cooking during winter when it is too cold to have the kitchen door or windows opened while cooking.

Some kitchen extractors need replacement. Remember to change your cloth after cooking to avoid smelling like fish in bed with your husband.

God will help us all in Jesus' mighty name. Woman, never give up on yourself, because God will never give up on you. Take good care of yourself. Look good, smell good and open your mouth with wisdom. Be the Proverbs 31 woman.

5. **Be an asset and not a liability**. Some people say it is not good for a woman to build houses. I do not know exactly what they are saying. If it is an agreement between the husband and wife to have things in common because they are one in marriage, then so be it. If the husband does not mind, why not! The Proverbs 31 woman considered a land and bought it.

In whose name, I do not know. She was a merchant, a hard working woman who had no place for idleness.
She had no time to gossip around. She was so mindful of the state of her home to the point that her husband was not afraid. He could sit at the gate to discuss with men of high integrity. How confident about you is your man when he is outside?

If every financial need must wait for your husband to come back from his journey, then you are not the Proverb 31 woman. You must be able to solve some little financial issues while your husband is away on a business trip.

Be financially independent. Your children will respect you for that.

6. **Be a prudent wife**. Do not spend the money set aside for the family to buy designer bags and shoes that have no second hand value. Help to invest the family finances well. Pray before involving yourself in any investment. Not all investment ideas are good ideas. I had a terrible experience some years ago. Do not go that way. Seek God's face and be in agreement with your husband.

7. You are a woman of great value. Do not let lack of wisdom turn you to what God has not made you to be.
You are God's best choice to bring forth the saviour of the whole world just like Mary the mother of Jesus.
You are highly favoured in Jesus' mighty name.
Remain blessed and be the woman God has created you to be.
Your home will not be inhabited by any strange woman in Jesus' name. Amen.
PRAISE THE LORD.

Confession For The Woman

I am a woman of God.
I have the Spirit of God in me.
My husband shall be satisfied with my breast alone.
The voice of a strange woman, my husband will not hear in Jesus' name.
My husband shall be enraptured with my Love.
My husband's left hand will be under my head and his right hand will embrace me.
The Songs of Solomon 6:8-9 talks about sixty queens, eighty concubines and virgins without number. But my dove, my perfect one, is the only one.
I will be the only woman called his wife in Jesus' mighty name.
God made us one in marriage and so shall it be in Jesus' mighty name.
There shall be no crack in my marriage in Jesus' mighty name.
I will enjoy my marriage to the fullest and my children and children's children will be blessed of the Lord in Jesus' mighty name. Amen.

Confession for the man

I am a man of purpose,
Created in the image of God.
God has made me to be the head of my home and so shall I be.
God has called me to be the Prophet of my home and I will not be a failure in this assignment.
I will not be reduced to crumbs of bread by a strange woman.
My labour in life and marriage will not be for another man to enjoy.
I shall be who God says I am in marriage and destiny.
I will be the head and not the tail.
I will be a man of God's wisdom and understanding.
I will fear and worship the God of heaven.
He will be the head of my marital life.
I will be a faithful servant to God in my marriage.
Destinies shall be fulfilled in my marriage and
I will be a true lover to the wife of my youth in Jesus' mighty Name.

Amen.

Prayer of Salvation

In John 2:1-10, Jesus and His disciples were invited to a wedding in Cana of Galilee. During the ceremony, the couple ran out of wine and sought help from Jesus. New wine was made available by the wisdom of Christ Jesus. No matter how low the wine in your marriage is, you can still enjoy newness in your marital relationship by inviting Jesus Christ into your home.

If you would like to invite Him into your life and home, please say the following prayer with me:
"Lord Jesus, I come to you today as a sinner.
I confess that You are the Son of God.
I believe that You died on the cross for my sins and You rose from the dead.
I ask that You cleanse me with Your blood and forgive all my sins.
From today, I declare You as my Lord and my Saviour.
Satan, you have no hold on me. I am a new creation; I am born again in Jesus' Name.
Amen."

CPSIA information can be obtained
at www.ICGtesting.com
Printed in the USA
LVOW10s0743120917
548266LV00004B/7/P